LIFESKILLS IN ACTION

D1262337

Opening a Bank Account

SUSAN
ROSE SIMMS

LIFESKILLS IN ACTION

MONEY SKILLS

MONEY

Living on a Budget | Road Trip
Opening a Bank Account | The Guitar
Managing Credit | High Cost
Using Coupons | Get the Deal
Planning to Save | Something Big

LIVING

Renting an Apartment
Finding Transportation
Planning a Trip to the Grocery Store
Keeping It Clean: Household Chores
Cooking Your Own Meals

JOB

Preparing a Résumé
Finding a Job
Job Interview Basics
How to Act Right on the Job
Employee Rights

SADDLEBACK
EDUCATIONAL PUBLISHING
www.sdlback.com

ISBN-13: 978-1-68021-005-7
ISBN-10: 1-68021-005-X
eBook: 978-1-63078-295-5

3 4873 00522 4357

Printed in Singapore by Craft Print International Ltd
0000/CA00000000

19 18 17 16 15   1 2 3 4 5

Ray calls his girlfriend, Elle. He knows she will not be happy. "I cannot go to the mall," he says.

"Why not?" Elle asks. "It's Saturday. We are all going."

"Not me," says Ray. "I am going to the bank."

"A bank? Why?"

Ray thinks back. Two months ago, he had big plans. Summer had started. Ray had many jobs.

He mowed Mr. Frank's lawn. He washed Mrs. Lee's car. The Halls took a long trip. They left their dog at home. Ray fed it every day. He walked it too.

Ray got paid. Mr. Frank paid him every week. Mrs. Lee paid him twice a month. The Halls paid him when they got back.

Ray wanted to save the money. He had plans for it. There is a guitar he really wants. It costs $400.

Ray had an idea. He put the money in a big envelope. He kept it in his closet. It was on a shelf. It was high.

Ray was sure that would work. "I cannot see it. I will not spend it." That is what Ray said.

But Ray was wrong. He could still reach the money. And things came up.

Ed and Ray are best friends. Ed lives next door. They hang out a lot. One day, Ed held up his phone. "Check out this cool band," he said. "Here is their new song."

"Okay," said Ray.

Ed played the song. Ray liked the beat. "I will buy it," he said.

His money was up in the closet. He could reach it. Ray bought a gift card. He got the new song. He bought four others too.

Elle likes to go out. She did not work all summer. Ray did. Elle missed him. She made plans.

"You are always busy. Let's go out tonight. Let's see a movie," said Elle.

"Okay," said Ray.

His money was there. He could reach it. He planned to put it back.

Ray took Elle to the movie. He bought two tickets. He got drinks. He got popcorn. He did not put the money back.

Chang is Ray's friend. He is popular. He likes to look good.

One day, Chang called. "I need new shades," he said. "But I do not have any money. Loan me the money, man. I know you have some."

Ray wanted to help Chang. He did not say no. But Chang never paid him back.

Ray still wants that guitar. But his plan did not work. The money was too easy to grab. He spent it all.

Ray's parents knew about his plans. Two weeks ago, they were all eating dinner. "How are your jobs?" asked Ray's mom. "Are you saving for your guitar?"

Ray looked sad. "I do want that guitar," he said. "But I have no money."

His dad looked surprised. "Where is all the money you made?"

"I do not have it. It is hard to save money. I spent it all."

That night his mom and dad talked. They had an idea. They wanted to help Ray.

The next day they talked to Ray. "Find a bank. Put your money there. Save half of what you need. We will match the other half."

Ray wants that guitar. This sounded like a good deal.

"You save $200," said his mom.

"Then we will add $200," said his dad.

"Nice!" said Ray. "Thanks."

Ray was happy. He knew he could do it. He just needed to find a bank.

"I can ask my sister," thought Ray. "She has a job. She goes to a bank."

His sister told him things. "Go online. Check out the banks. Make sure they have a site. You will want to be able to log in. You will want to bank online."

"Thanks," said Ray.

Ray and Pete are friends. Pete uses a credit union. Ray asked why.

Pete said, "I chose the credit union. I like it better than banks. It does not have a lot of fees."

Ray talked to his parents. "What do you like about your bank?"

They told him things. "It is close to home," said his mom.

"They have an app for my phone. I can deposit a check with it," said his dad.

"What do you want from your bank?" they asked Ray.

"I want an ATM machine," said Ray. "I want to be able to take money out. I want to put money in. The machine is open 24 hours. I like that."

"What else?"

"Free checking," said Ray.

"What about savings?" asked his dad. "You want to save for that guitar."

"That is important," said Ray.

"Some banks charge for a low balance," said his mom.

"I do not want that," said Ray.

Ray thought about all this. He went online. He typed the words "teen" and "bank" in the search box. A lot of links came up.

Ray saw many ads. He looked for ads with teens. One bank had "Money 101 for Teens." Ray read about saving. He read about interest rates.

One credit union had student checking. It was free. There was no set amount to start. There was no set amount to keep in.

"Take your time, son," said his mom.

"Make a good choice," said his dad.

"I will," said Ray. "I have a plan."

The two weeks went by. Ray talked to his mom and dad.

"I chose my bank," he said. He went on. "I found two good banks. I made a list. I wrote things I liked. I wrote things I did not like."

"That was a good plan," said his mom.

"I saw them side by side. I saw the one I liked."

"Okay," said his dad. "Tomorrow we will go to your bank."

It is Saturday. Ray calls Elle. He tells her he cannot go to the mall. He and his dad are going to the bank. Ray is ready to open an account.

Ray has his permit. He drives. His dad sits next to him. "It is close," says his dad.

"It is easy to get to," says Ray.

They get to the bank. They go inside. A man greets them. He shakes hands with Ray.

"It is nice to meet you," says Ray.

They sit down. The man looks at Ray. "What can I do for you?"

"I want to open an account," says Ray. "I will start with $20."

There are papers to sign. Then the man hands something to Ray.

"Here is a book, Ray. It's called a register. Use it to keep track of your money. Write what you put in. Write what you take out."

Ray gets two books. One is for checking. One is for savings.

"This shows how much money you have," says his dad. "Do not spend more than you have."

"Set up your account online," says the banker. "Go to the website. Make a password. Keep it secret."

Ray asks about the ATM. "How do I use it?"

"Here is a card," the man says. "Choose four numbers. No one else should know them."

"Do not tell your friends," says his dad. "It is your PIN. It is for the card. Only you should know it."

The man nods. "Your dad is right. Keep your PIN secret."

The man smiles at Ray. "Come in the bank if you have questions. The tellers can help. They are at the counter."

"Thank you," says Ray. They shake hands.

Ray is happy. Now he can save for the guitar. His money is in a safe place.

"I will save that $200," says Ray. "That guitar will be mine."

Will opening an account help Ray save? Did he ask the right questions when he chose his bank? Want to find out more about opening an account?

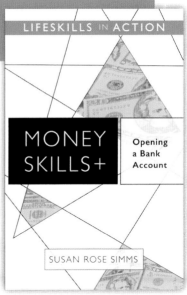

LIFESKILLS IN ACTION

MONEY SKILLS+

Opening a Bank Account

SUSAN ROSE SIMMS

JUST *flip* THE BOOK!

The Guitar

SUSAN ROSE SIMMS

LIFESKILLS IN ACTION
MONEY SKILLS

SADDLEBACK
EDUCATIONAL PUBLISHING
www.sdlback.com

ISBN-13: 978-1-68021-005-7
ISBN-10: 1-68021-005-X
eBook: 978-1-63078-295-5

Printed in Singapore by Craft Print International Ltd
0000/CA00000000

19 18 17 16 15 1 2 3 4 5

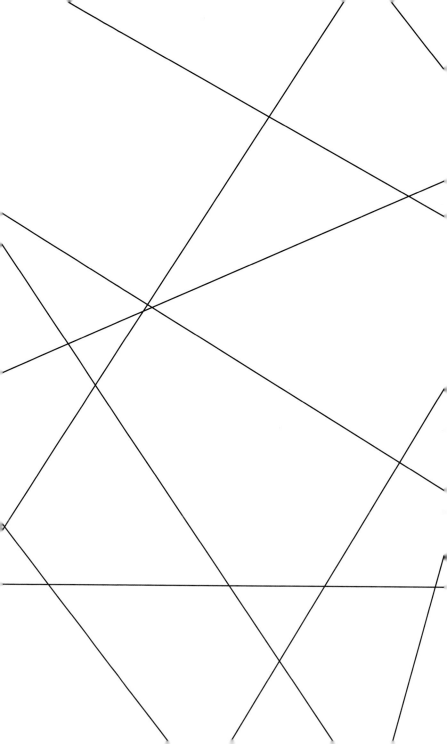

Money.

It is easy to spend. But it can be hard to keep track of.

You think you have some. Then you look. Your wallet is empty. You think back. You went to a game last week. The tickets cost money. So did the food. You spent all your cash there.

How do you keep track of your money?

Many people get help.

From a **bank**. Or a **credit union**.

These places keep money safe.

You put money in. They keep track of it for you.

How? Just open an account.

Bank Account Application

Where should you open an **account**?

It is your money. You must decide where to put it.

A **bank** is a business. It has owners. They want to make money.

So banks charge **fees**. Fees bring in money.

Many banks are big. They have places all over the U.S.

That is nice if you travel. Or go away to college.

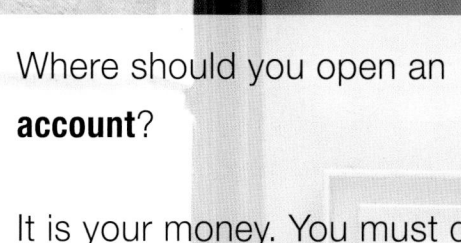

self-service

A **credit union** is small. It is in one city or state. A few are in more than one state.

It is made for a group of people. You have to be in the group to join.

People who join are members. They own the credit union.

Credit unions charge fees too. But not as many as banks.

And the fees are often lower.

6

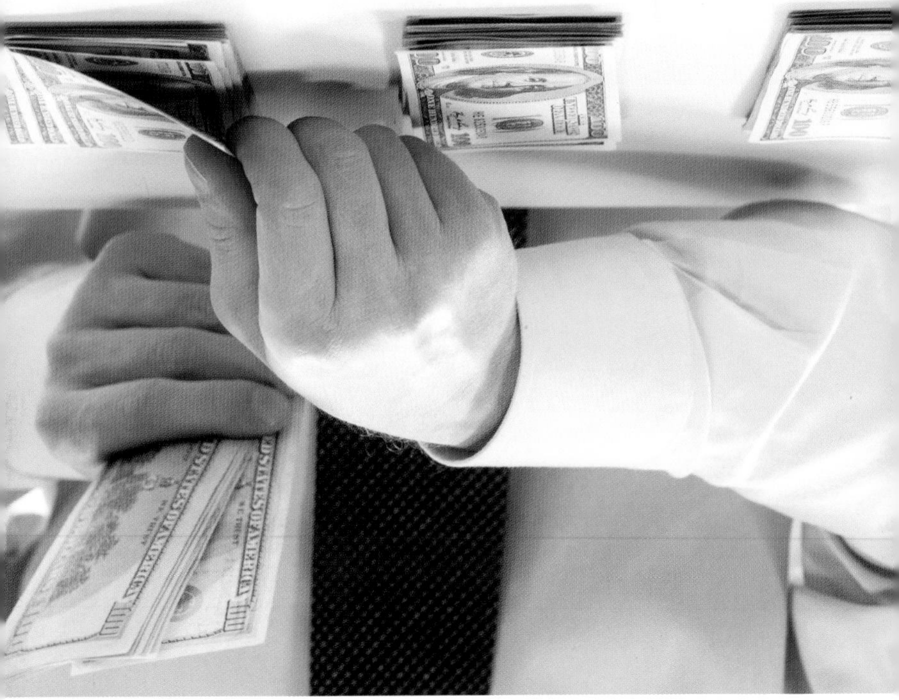

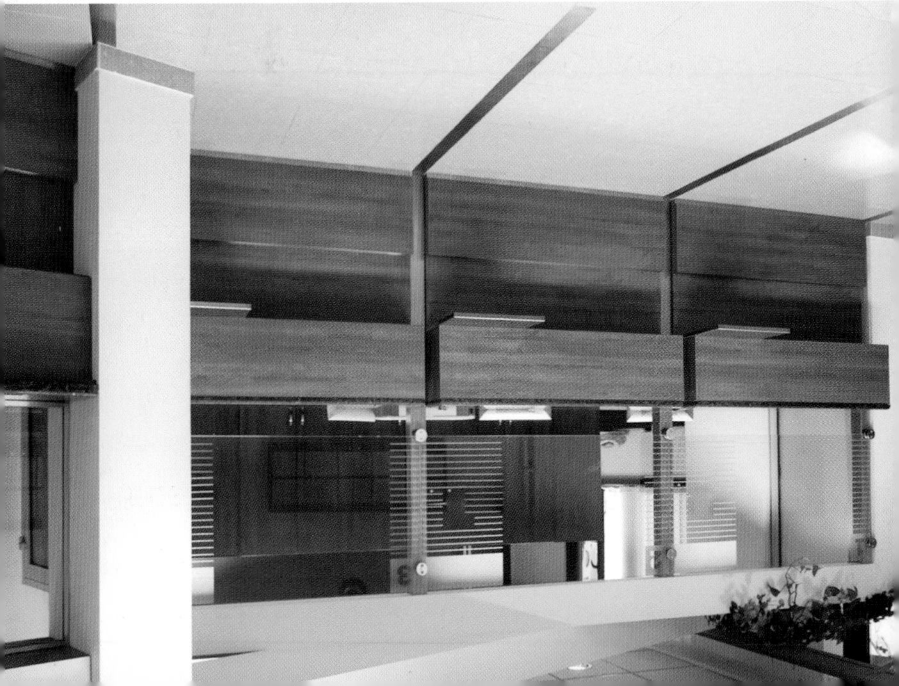

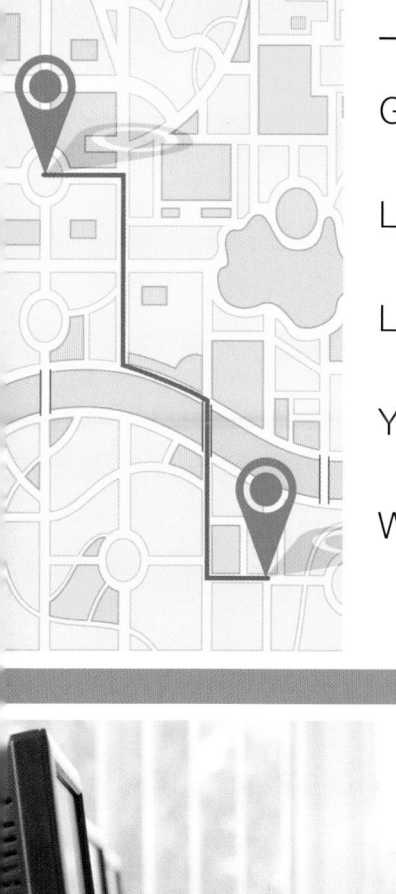

Go online.

Look for banks near you.

Look for credit unions too.

You will find many.

Which one is for you?

HERE ARE SOME THINGS TO THINK ABOUT:

- When is it open? Does it have 24-hour ATMs?

- Is the account free? Or is there a fee?

- How much money do you need to open an account?

- Can you bank with your phone?

11

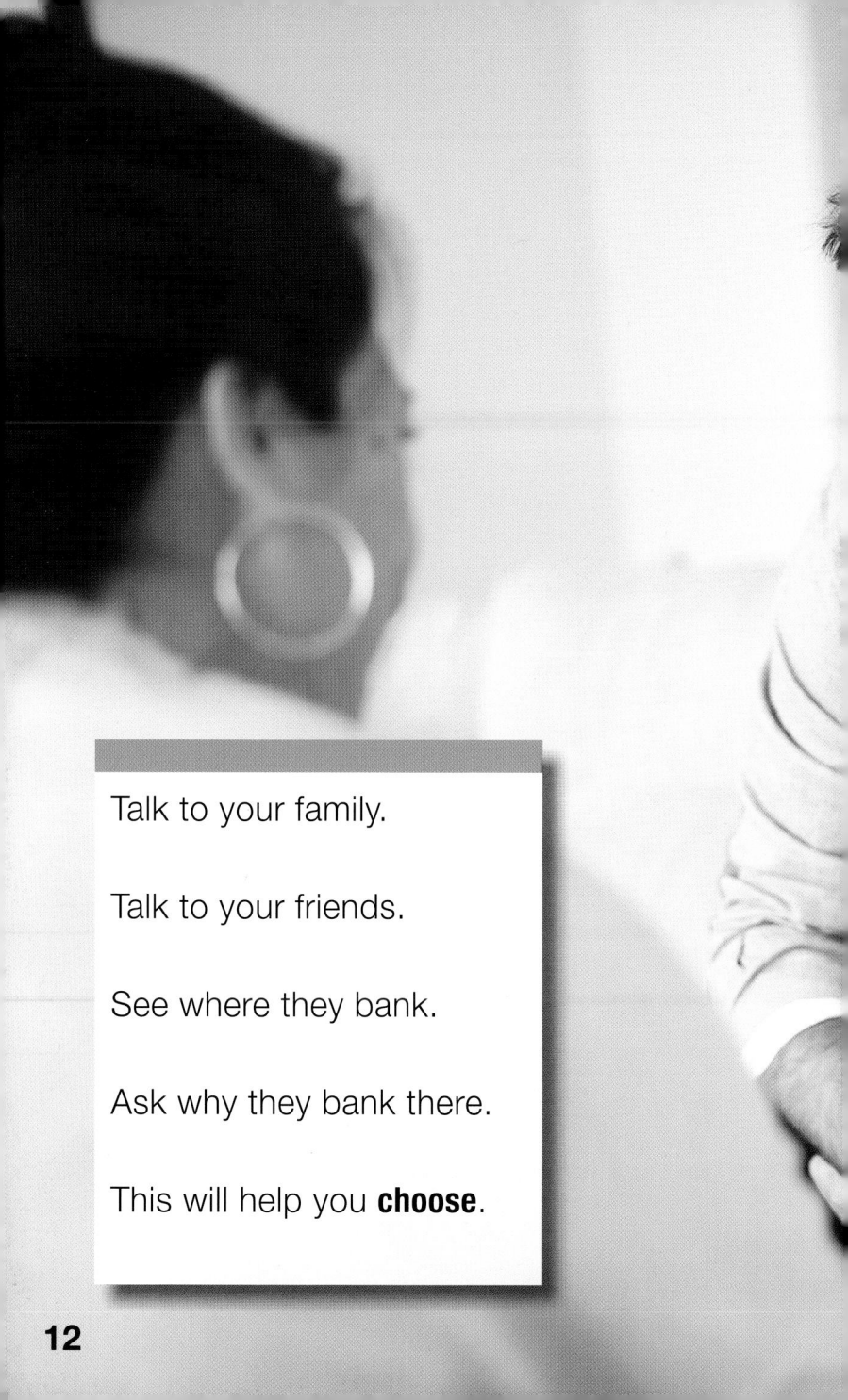

Talk to your family.

Talk to your friends.

See where they bank.

Ask why they bank there.

This will help you **choose**.

Are you ready to open an account?

You must be 18 to go by yourself.

Are you under 18?

Then a parent must come with you.

You will fill out a form. **Sign** your name.

Your parent will sign too.

You need a **photo ID**.

This can be your school ID card.

It can be a driver's permit. Or license.

It can be a passport.

Have your **social security number**. You will need that too.

Bring money with you.

You will need it to open your account.

It can be cash.

Or it can be a check made out to you.

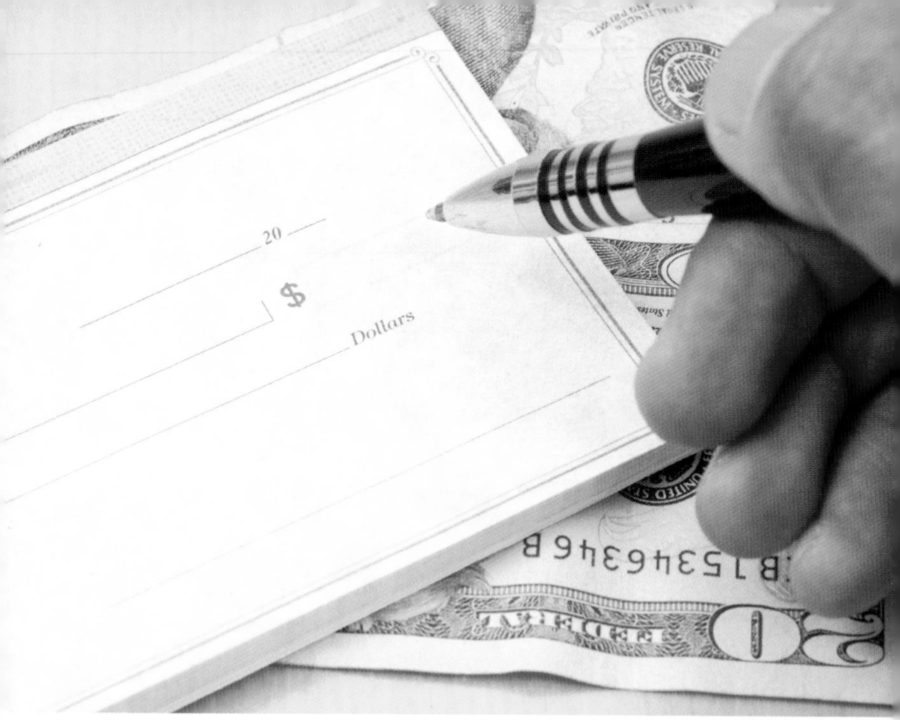
20
$
Dollars
B15346346B
FEDERAL

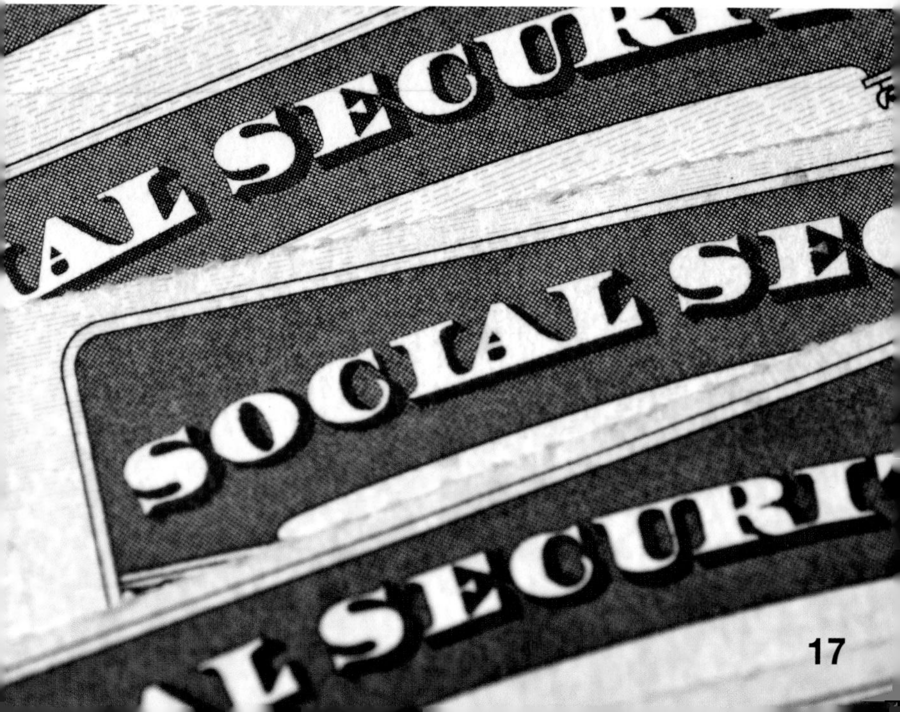
SOCIAL SECURITY

Now you need to decide.

What kind of account do you want?

It depends on what you plan to do with your money.

Are you keeping money to spend later?

A **savings account** is good for that.

Your money will be safe.

It will even earn a bit of money.

This is called **interest**.

You can take money out of savings.

But the idea is to let it grow.

Add more money as you make it.

What if you want to spend your money?

You want to keep track of it.

But it must be easy to get. Easy to spend.

This is what a **checking account** is for.

It is easy to take money out of checking.

The bank keeps track for you.

You will see where the money goes.

Think about your money.

You may want to spend some.

You may want to save some too.

Open two accounts.

One can be checking. The other can be savings.

Did you open a checking account?

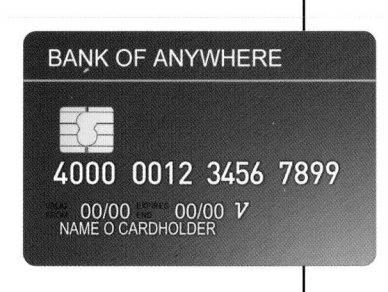

Ask about a **debit card**.

It makes it easy to get money.

Use it to pay for things. The money comes out of your account.

How does the card work? It has a secret code.

This is called a **PIN**. A personal identification number.

You can use the card at a store.

You can use it online.

You can use it at an ATM.

But you must enter your PIN.

The card will not work without it.

Keep your PIN secret. Do not give it out.
Not even to a friend.

Help keep your money safe.

You will also get paper **checks**.

You fill these out to pay for things.
You sign your name.

There is a small book. It comes with the
checks.

It is called a **register**. You write in it.

You will take money out. You will put
money in.

Write it all down.

Know how much money you have.

A check can **bounce**.

That means you do not have the money.

You write a check for $75. You only have $65 in the bank.

The check will not work. There will be a fee. It can cost you a lot.

You will get a **statement**.

There is one each month.

It shows all the money in.

It lists all the money out.

Look for it in the mail. Or get it online.

Check the statement. Look at
your register.

The money should be the same.

BANK STATEMENT
FOR THE MONTH ENDED JULY 31

DEPOSITS AND CREDITS

CHECKS AND DEBITS

DEPOSITS AND CREDITS	CHECKS AND DEBITS
300.00	
1,250.00	
	1,100.00
993.60	415.20
	10.00
1,023.77	
	400.00
1,5	.00
	4,095.75

26

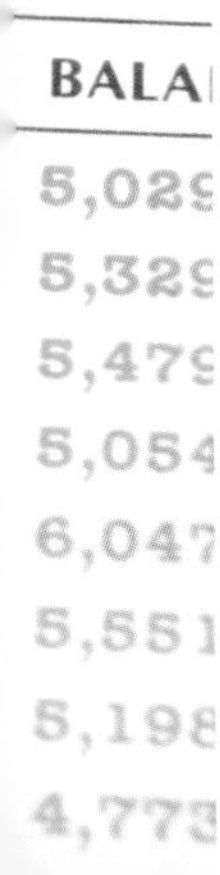

If not, find out why.

Did you take money out? Did you forget to write it down? Fix that.

Did the bank make a mistake? If so, report it.

BALA

5,029
5,329
5,479
5,054
6,047
5,551
5,198
4,773

You have your account. Keep up with it **online**.

Set up your name. Make a password.

Do not tell anyone what it is.

Sign in. Check how much money you have.

You can do more online. You can pay bills.

You can also move your money.

This is called a **transfer**.

Do you need money to pay a bill? Take money from savings. Put it in checking.

Do you want to save more? Take money from checking. Put it in savings.

Money.

You want to keep it **safe**.

You need to keep track of it.

Make it easy.

Open a bank account.

Your money will be safe.

And you can spend it when you need it.

31

What makes a teen want to open a bank account? You'll see why Ray decides he needs one in *The Guitar*. Want to read on?

SUSAN ROSE SIMMS

The Guitar

JUST *flip* THE BOOK!